Loving and Serving Others
The Practice of Risk-Taking Mission and Service

Robert Schnase

ABINGDON PRESS
Nashville

Loving and Serving Others:
The Practice of Risk-Taking Mission and Service
All rights reserved.

Originally appeared in *Five Practices of Fruitful Living* by Robert Schnase,
which was published by Abingdon Press in 2010.

ISBN 978-1-6308-8304-1

All Scripture quotations, unless otherwise indicated, are taken from the
New Revised Standard Version of the Bible, copyright 1989, Division of
Christian Education of the National Council of the Churches of Christ in the
United States of America. Used by permission. All rights reserved.

Scripture quotations noted (*The Message*) are from THE MESSAGE.
Copyright © by Eugene H. Peterson 1993, 1994, 1995, 1996, 2000, 2001, 2002.
Used by permission of NavPress Publishing Group.

14 15 16 17 18 19 20 21 22 23--10 9 8 7 6 5 4 3 2 1
MANUFACTURED IN THE UNITED STATES OF AMERICA

Contents

The Fruitful Living Series 5

Why Serve Others? 17

An Essential Truth 33

Training the Heart 51

Social Witness 69

Leader Helps 87

Notes 96

Loving and Serving Others
The Practice of Risk-Taking Mission and Service

Then Jesus went to work on his disciples. . . . "Don't run from suffering; embrace it. Follow me and I'll show you how. Self-help is no help at all. Self-sacrifice is the way, my way, to finding yourself, your true self."
—*Matthew 16:24-25*, The Message

The Fruitful Living Series

Jesus taught a way of life and invited people into a relationship with God that was vibrant, dynamic, and fruitful. He said, "I am the vine, you are the branches. Those who abide in me and I in them bear much fruit.... My father is glorified by this, that you bear much fruit and become my disciples," (John 15: 5, 8). Jesus wanted people to flourish.

Scripture is sprinkled with phrases that point to fruitful living—the kingdom of God, eternal life, immeasurable riches, a peace that passes all understanding, abundant life.

How do I cultivate a life that is abundant, fruitful, purposeful, and deep? What are the commitments, critical risks, and practices that open me to God's transforming grace and that help me discover the difference God intends for me to make in the world?

How do I live the fruitful, flourishing life of a follower of Christ?

Radical Hospitality. Passionate Worship. Intentional Faith Development. Risk-Taking Mission and Service. Extravagant Generosity.

Since the publication of *Five Practices of Fruitful Congregations,* these edgy, provocative, dangerous words have helped hundreds of congregations understand their mission, renew ministries, and stretch toward fruitfulness and excellence for the purposes of Christ.

The Fruitful Living Series moves the discussion of Christian practice from the congregational level to the personal practices of discipleship. The fruitful God-related life develops with intentional and repeated attention to five essential practices that are critical for our growth in Christ.

Radical Hospitality in our personal walk with Christ begins with an extraordinary receptivity to the grace of God. In distinctive and personal ways, we invite God into our hearts and make space for God in our lives. We receive God's love and offer it to others.

Through the practice of *Passionate Worship*, we learn to love God in return. We practice listening to God, allowing God to shape our hearts and minds through prayer, personal devotion, and community worship. We love God.

Through the practice of *Intentional Faith Development*, we do the soul work that connects us to others, immerses us in God's word, and positions us to grow in grace and mature in Christ. We learn in community.

The practice of *Risk-Taking Mission and Service* involves offering ourselves in purposeful service to others in need,

making a positive difference even at significant personal cost and inconvenience to our own lives. We serve.

Through the practice of *Extravagant Generosity*, we offer our material resources in a manner that supports the causes that transform life and relieve suffering and that enlarges the soul and sustains the spirit. We give back.

These five practices—to receive God's love, to love God in return, to grow in Christ, to serve others, and to give back—are so essential to growth in Christ and to the deepening of the Spiritual life that failure to attend to them, develop them, and deepen them with intentionality limits our capacity to live fruitfully and fully, to settle ourselves completely in God, and to become instruments of God's transforming grace. The adjectives—*radical, passionate, intentional, risk-taking,* and *extravagant*—provoke us out of complacency and remind us that these practices require more than haphazard, infrequent, and mediocre attention.

These practices open our heart—to God, to others, to a life that matters, a life rich with meaning, relationship, and contribution. They help us flourish.

Christian Practice

The ministry of Jesus is grounded in personal practices. Jesus' life is marked by prayer, solitude, worship, reflection, the study of scripture, conversation, community, serving, engagement with suffering, and generosity. These personal practices sustained a ministry that opened people to God's grace, transformed human hearts, and changed the circumstances of people in need.

Christian practices are those essential activities we repeat and deepen over time. They create openings for God's spirit to shape us. Practices are not simply principles we talk about; practices are something we do. They make our faith a tangible and visible part of daily life. We see them

done in the life of Jesus, and we do them until they become a way of life for us. We become instruments of God's grace and love.

Through practice, we open ourselves to grace and let ourselves be opened by grace. We follow Christ, step by step, day by day, again and again; and by these steps and through these days, we are changed, we become someone different, we become new creations in Christ.

The books in this series are based on the premise that by repeating and deepening certain fundamental practices, we cooperate with God in our own growth in Christ and participate with the Holy Spirit in our own spiritual maturation. The fundamental practices are rooted in scripture and derived from the clear imperatives of the life of Christ. This isn't a self-improvement, pull-yourself-up-by-your-own-bootstraps notion of how we grow in grace. It's not about trying harder, working longer, or striving more to achieve God's blessing.

The Christian life is a gift of God, an expression of God's grace in Christ, the result of an undeserved and unmerited offering of love toward us. Every step of the journey toward Christ is preceded by, made possible by, and sustained by the perfecting grace of God.

The fruitful life is cultivated by placing ourselves in the most advantageous places to see, receive, learn, and understand the love that has been offered in Christ.

How to Use *The Fruitful Living Series*

The Fruitful Living Series is deeply personal, and as such it is composed of stories—the experiences, hopes, doubts, good efforts, and false starts of people like you and me. Faith journeys are used to illustrate key points so as to encourage honest reflection and conversation. But the approach is not individualistic—only about me, my, and mine. Every experience embeds us more deeply in the community of Christ because it is in the presence of our sisters and brothers that our spirits are sustained, our hearts encouraged.

I pray for those who reach for these books searching for understanding about their own faith journeys, that it may stimulate them to deeper life in Christ. But I pray especially for those who have been handed these books and who open their pages reluctantly, that they may open themselves to the possibility that something in the stories and reflections

may cause them to think more deeply, pray more earnestly, and serve others in a more fruitful and satisfying way.

This series is experiential rather than systematic or dogmatic. It relies on the experiences of ordinary people who have been extraordinarily shaped by their relationship to God. None of us has the complete picture. Movement toward Christ is never a straight line, uninterrupted, obstacle free, totally consistent, predictable and easily describable. There are no perfect accounts that capture everything that lies behind and no completely reliable maps that outline the future in one's faith journey. Soul work is hard, and following Christ is messy, challenging, joyous, scary, painful, sustaining, and frustratingly indescribable.

This *Fruitful Living Series* is about the everyday faith of everyday people seeking to listen for God, to love each other, to care for those in need, to embrace the stranger, to live the fruit of the spirit.

These books are practical. They are about what we do daily and intentionally, and about who we become because of how God uses what we do. They suggest a compass rather than map; a direction helpful for many diverse contexts rather than a specific step-by-step, how-to plan that fits only certain terrain.

Engage the material personally. Discover what you can learn about yourself, your relationship with God, your personal desires and internal resistances in the life of faith.

And read *The Fruitful Living Series* with others on the journey to Christ. Use it in house groups, adult Sunday school classes, a weeknight book study, or with your family. Resolve to deepen your own practices of faith. Pray for one another and support one another in Christ. Encourage church leaders and pastors to use the book in retreats, sermons series, or evening studies. These five focus the essential work that forms disciples; by cultivating these practices in the lives of those reached by the community

of faith, the congregation fulfills its mission of making disciples of Jesus Christ for the transformation of the world.

As a pastor and bishop, I've been granted the privilege of witnessing people whose faith is immeasurably greater than my own, whose sacrifice more than I myself could ever bear, whose impact in the lives of others through their service is immeasurably more than mine, whose personal discipline, depth of spirit, and maturing in Christ is far ahead of anything I shall ever achieve or hope to receive, and whose generosity is so extraordinary that it humbles me completely. This book is about how we learn from their fruitfulness in Christ so that we cooperate with God in becoming what God created us to be.

My prayer for you and your congregation is that *The Fruitful Living Series* helps us all grow in grace and in the knowledge and love of God. May we be changed from the inside out so that we can transform the world for the purposes of Christ.

Loving and Serving Others

WHY SERVE OTHERS?

> *For those who want to save their lives will lose it, and those who lose their life for my sake, and for the sake of the gospel, will save it.*
> —Mark 8:35

"Why would I want to do that?" Brad asked, at the prospect of getting up early on Saturday morning to join others from the church to prepare lunch for the homeless at a soup kitchen. "I've got my own things going on. I need time for myself and my family. And besides, what difference is it going to make, anyway?"

I've heard those questions spoken by others, and to be honest, I wrestle with them myself. They are not questions of planning and time management, but of spirit, focus, and purpose.

We live to ourselves. It is comfortable, safe, and natural to do so. We take care of our own. Instinct. Self-preservation. Love of family. Cocooning. Enjoying the fruits of our labor. These are important, and we don't need unearned guilt for wanting to rest on the weekend.

Each of us has a whole world of private concerns, personal passions, hobbies, entertainments, family responsibilities, and work obligations. The circle in which we live, work, and play is small, but intense, and important. And it is ours.

Why give the time or make the effort to reach beyond our world to serve other people? And would it make any real difference, anyway?

Since time immemorial, prophets and religious leaders, philosophers and poets, reformers and civic leaders have taught the importance of helping those in need and directing our lives outward to make a difference in the world. They remind us to act with kindness, gentleness, and self-control in our everyday lives in the way we regard strangers. They teach us to interrupt our routines and suffer inconvenience to aid those who are in temporary distress, to tend the injured, comfort the bereaved, feed the hungry. They call us to more deliberate efforts to relieve suffering, protect the vulnerable, and respond to the human trauma of natural disasters with compassion and assistance. They prompt us to address social change, to confront unjust systems, to direct resources toward eliminating disease, and to hold purveyors of violence to accountability. A critical key to a life that is rich in purpose and that, in the end, we find satisfying, involves serving other people and

making a positive difference in the world around us. But why is that? Why should we serve others? Why help?

This ethical consensus conflicts with other messages and myths that pervade our culture. "Look out for number one." "Love yourself first." "If we all pursue our own self-interests, the collective results help everyone thrive." "Helping people in need feeds dependency and squelches initiative." "It's survival of the fittest." "Taking care of me, my own family, and my own community comes first." "People are responsible for their own misfortunes." "Trying to help everyone takes us all down, and sinks the lifeboat." "It's not my problem." "One person's efforts make no real difference at all."

These attitudes influence us, even if we seldom articulate them so pointedly. Sometimes we act as if we believe that if we merely focus on our own personal circle—our work, our family, our homes—that the great issues of human suffering do not impact us, and that we have no role or responsibility. To avoid, deny, ignore, or blame others for the causes of suffering helps us live a carefree, less anxious life.

"Most people, given the choice between having a better world, or a better place within the world as it is, would choose the latter." This cynical analysis of the human condition, attributed to Ralph W. Sockman, captures the magnitude of the issue. Our energy naturally goes to making a better place for ourselves.

Society convinces us that this is the best way to care for ourselves and our families.

So, why serve others? Why work for a better world?

First, some people serve others out of a sense of duty, obligation, and responsibility. Helping others is imperative, and they serve others without regard to the personal cost or inconvenience. If the church needs volunteers at the soup kitchen, they show up. If a community agency needs coats for the poor, they dig through their closets and give what they can. When a hurricane devastates coastal homes, they contribute generously. Being part of the church team means they wear the uniform, show up for practice, and offer their best, and some become quite skilled at the tasks of helping others.

Imagine how it would change your life to take Jesus' commands seriously and to cultivate such trust that when Jesus says "do it," you would respond with complete and utter obedience. Jesus tells us to feed the hungry, clothe the naked, visit the imprisoned, welcome the stranger. Many people take those words at face value, and offer their best and highest, trusting that whether they enjoy the work or not, these are the right things to do. Following the imperatives of Christ becomes a way of life they adopt whole-heartedly. I've known lay prison chaplains, volunteers at homeless shelters, tutors of underprivileged children, directors of medical clinics, and workers with addicts for whom their initial motivation was simple and obvious: "Jesus tells me to do it, and so I do it."

Whatever inner spiritual work, personal passion, or satisfaction they enjoy are after-the-fact results of the activity rather than motivations that initially draw them in. Never underestimate the impact of people motivated by duty.

Second, there are those who serve because helping others contributes to the social fabric of human life. Living in this world requires an unspoken social contract that requires me to help you when you need it, trusting that you will help me when I need it.

Serving greases the machinery of social interaction and creates a sustainable mutuality that is essential for co-existence. If I care for you and you care for me, then both of us find ourselves cared for.

This motivation surfaces after catastrophes and natural disasters. People imagine their own home flooded, their own house on fire, their own school struck by violence, and they think of how devastating that would be and how deeply helpful the community would become for them. They gather around, and offer their best, even across great distances. However, the more remote the need, the more difficult it is to see the interconnections and the reciprocities that motivate courageous action to help. While I may be able to imagine my home burning down and temporarily

depending upon other people, I may not be able to see myself as a homeless addict living on the streets of the inner city, or as a refugee starving in a camp on a foreign desert and so I may not see the connection between their lives and mine.

Third, some people discover that serving provides immeasurable personal satisfaction for themselves. They like the way it feels to know that the work they have done, a project they have sponsored, or a policy they have supported has truly relieved suffering, or improved the conditions of people in need. As one person says, "I like myself better and I'm happier when I help others in concrete ways." Making a difference enriches our lives, adds an element of enchantment and adventure and satisfaction that other activities cannot match.

The Holy Spirit purifies all of these motivations when we serve others with the right spirit and focus genuinely on meeting human needs in ways that respect recipients and serve the purposes of Christ.

Need-focused service and passion-driven commitment do not necessarily conflict. In *Wishful Thinking*, Frederick Buechner describes God's call to service and ministry as "the place where your deep gladness and the world's deep hunger meet."[1]

Picture a graph-like matrix. Along the left side of the graph are all the deep human needs, sufferings, and challenges that require bold and courageous service. These are the things God needs people to work on.

Along the bottom of the graph are all the particular gifts and passions that characterize our life. These things personally motivate us. Somewhere on the graph, unmet needs intersect with our own personal passions, and that's where we find ourselves offering effective help. That's where we take our place in God's service, making a difference in ways we find satisfying.

If someone responds only to needs for which they have no passion, they work slave-like for purposes that do not compel them.

On the other hand, if they disregard the world's needs, and only do what they want to do, then they risk offering ministry that is irrelevant for God's purposes, and they serve themselves rather than responding to God's call.

Out of Touch with Reality?

Philosophers ponder the question of why a stranger walking by a burning building and hearing the cry of someone inside would put his life at risk to enter the building to try to save a person he does not know.

Think about this with me. The stranger who responds puts everything on the line in that moment. He places at risk his entire future—seeing his children graduate and grow to adulthood, holding in his hands his own grandchildren, decades of future earnings and support for his family, years of affectionate partnership with his wife, all that he might accomplish at work and in the community for the remainder of his natural life. In a split-second decision to enter the burning building, he puts all this at risk for a person he does not know and without regard as to whether

the person deserves it or not, is healthy or sick, lives with riches or in poverty, or whether the person's prospects for the future are positive or negative. Why does he do it? Is he out of touch with reality?

In that critical moment of pure insight and absolute choice, the person *is not out of touch with reality*. In that moment the person *perceives the truest reality* of all, that our lives are interconnected, that our futures are intertwined with one another, and that we are ultimately one. In moments of such revelation, we see so clearly that we are propelled to the highest and truest of responses. If I let you die, I kill something inside myself.

Ultimately people are not isolated egos, separate and self-absorbed, capable only of self-preservation. I do not live in a universe occupied only by myself. We are one; we belong to one body. In theological terms, you belong to me and I belong to you because we both belong to God. You are my sister or brother and I am yours because God gives both of us life and loves us both unconditionally and completely. God's grace laces our lives inextricably

together. When I perceive that reality, I can do no other than to try to help you. In the bold, risky, sacrificial action of entering a burning building to aid a stranger, we witness a raw distillation of the impulses toward what is true. We willingly pour ourselves out because no other way ultimately leads to life.

The deeper truth that we see so clearly in dramatic life-and-death events is one we intuitively perceive in our daily lives and non-critical moments, and this leads us to pour out our lives in small ways each day in service to our families, our children, our communities, and even to strangers. A well-lived life that is in touch with reality involves sacrificing ourselves in the daily care of our children, the love of a spouse, the care of a neighbor, and the service to strangers, each day giving parts of ourselves up and losing our lives for others. Nothing sustains the flourishing of life and spirit like genuinely pouring ourselves into the lives of others. This does not diminish life; it fulfills it. This is love.

On September 11, 2001, the United States experienced unfathomable pain and loss with the deaths of innocent

people. In the countless heroic stories of people who sacrificed their lives to save others, the world also perceived a glimpse of the reality of human connection that was sharper and more focused than we usually see. The tragedy provoked a reality check for countless people, causing them to explore profound questions, such as "Who am I? Who is important to me? How am I related to the people around me? What really matters?" In the brokenness, violence, and grief, we also saw more clearly than usual what is sustaining and trustworthy.

REFLECTION

For those who want to
SAVE THEIR LIFE
will **LOSE IT**,
and those who **LOSE THEIR LIFE**
for **MY SAKE,** *and for the*
SAKE OF THE GOSPEL,
will **SAVE** *it.*

—Mark 8:35

> *God calls you at "the place where your deep gladness and the world's deep hunger meet."*
> *—Frederick Buechner,* Wishful Thinking

Questions

- Who taught you to value serving others? How did you learn to serve? Who modeled the life of service for you?
- What's your earliest memory of helping others as an expression of your faith?
- What motivates you to serve, to relieve suffering, or to seek justice? Do you delight in doing good?
- What particular gifts, abilities, or experiences prepare you to make a positive difference personally or in your community?
- Where do the world's unmet needs intersect with your own personal passion?

Prayer

Help me forget myself enough to truly help others. Shape my worries into prayers and my prayers into practices that serve your purposes as I serve others.

Loving and Serving Others

AN ESSENTIAL TRUTH

Jesus said, "Whoever wants to be great must become a servant. . . . That is what the Son of Man has done: He came to serve, not be served—and then to give away his life. . ."
—Matthew 20:27-28, The Message

Hundreds of scriptural stories reveal this essential truth that our lives are interwoven, and that we discover ourselves fully in giving ourselves to others. Paul writes, "We do not live to ourselves, and we do not die to ourselves. If we live, we live to the Lord, and if we die, we die to the Lord; so then, whether we live or whether we die, we are the Lord's" (Romans 14:7-8).

Scripture suggests that to encounter Jesus Christ face-to-face in the most tangible way, the whole reality he embodies, involves serving another person by relieving suffering through feeding the hungry, clothing the naked, visiting the imprisoned, and welcoming the stranger. "I'm telling the solemn truth: Whenever you did one of these things to someone overlooked or ignored, that was me—you did it to me" (Matthew 25:40, *The Message*).

Serving others does not merely involve helpful activities that make a difference; Christ-like service helps us become the persons God created us to be. It fulfills God's hope and will for us.

Do we really believe that the ultimate revelation of the heart of God is the life, teachings, death, and resurrection of Jesus Christ? Was Jesus out of touch with reality when he embraced the lepers, interceded to protect the vulnerable, healed the blind, took the role of a servant and knelt before his disciples to wash their feet, welcomed the children, ate with tax collectors, told stories about a Samaritan assisting a foreigner, and taught his followers to visit the imprisoned? Or was Jesus in touch with the truest reality of all? Do we believe Jesus was leading us toward a flourishing life with these practices, or carelessly leading us astray?

By serving others, we bear witness that Jesus' reality is true, that fullness is discovered in the giving and not in the taking, that abundance is found in loving rather than in fearing, that happiness comes in opening ourselves rather than by closing ourselves off.

CHANGING THE WORLD

"When you change the world of a child,
you change the world."
—Anonymous

The real you, your true self, is discovered in letting Christ lead you into serving others with compassion. In serving, we mediate the grace of God. The unsolicited, unconditional love of God that we receive flows through us to others. God's purpose permeates us. As God's love runs through us, we see Jesus Christ more clearly; we work with him and he works through us. Serving puts Jesus' love into practice, and the ultimate reality we see in Christ becomes tangible once again, revealed as a force and power in the world. Serving others, we live the truth.

Separateness, suspicion, distance, fear, and estrangement pale when set alongside the generative, creative power of God's Spirit. We are made separate by fear; by grace, our lives are inextricably interwoven. We can serve out of sheer obedience or out of a sense of mutual obligation, or because we find meaning in it. The bottom line remains: in Christ, human suffering requires response.

Ultimately, the practice of compassionate service in Christ's name grows from interior decision, a spiritual reorientation. As our life with God becomes more vibrant,

dynamic, and real, we discover that we can choose to stand in a place of love, of hope, and of risk with an outward-focused posture; or we can choose to stand in a place of fear, defensiveness, protection, and self-absorption. Our hearts turn outward toward others and follow Jesus toward them, or we focus inwardly and away from others and go our own way. The more consciously aware we become of our interior life with God, the better choices we make. Growing closer to God draws us closer to one another.

Sifting through the motivations to serve takes place under a compelling and all-encompassing mandate, the reign of God. Prophets speak of the day when swords are beaten into plowshares, the wolf and lamb flourish together in peaceful coexistence, we no longer learn war, and the earth is full of the knowledge of God (Isaiah 2; 11). They speak of justice rolling down like waters, and righteousness like an ever-flowing stream (Amos 5:24). New Testament poetry teaches of lifting up the lowly and filling the hungry with good things (Luke 1:52-53). Jesus reveals God's intentions to bring good news to the poor, release to the captives, recovering of sight to the blind,

and setting free those who are oppressed (Luke 4:18). Jesus offers glimpses of the kingdom of God, visions of unexpected grace, surprising good news, renewed justice, abiding hope, and ever-present signs of new life. God reigns, and God pulls us toward the new creation. God is ahead, and that truth casts light on all things present. The future belongs to God, and to accept this interpretation of life changes how we think and act, lending hope, urgency, will, and courage to our efforts to follow Christ in serving others.

"Your kingdom come; Your will be done, on earth as it is in heaven." With this prayer, we offer ourselves afresh to the reign of God. We align toward God's intended future, we lean forward with hope, and we orient ourselves toward an end where all persons flourish, unrestrained by oppression, disease, or violence. We yearn with body, mind, and soul for the world God wills, and we offer ourselves toward the life God is preparing. We discover our calling to serve within the immeasurably vaster frame of God's purpose in reconciling the world to himself.

While many and various motivations *push us outward*, the kingdom of God *pulls us forward*, toward the compelling and glorious end of a world infused by God's love.

How we choose makes all the difference. Whom we trust to follow changes everything. What we believe about ultimate reality is pivotal. Meaningful, fruitful service involves the training of the heart. It begins with interior work. The story we choose to tell determines the life we choose to live.

On an impulse, someone contemplating the life and death of Jesus decided to lie down on her back on the grass of an open field with her arms totally stretched out as if on the cross. She remained in that position in a mood of exploring prayer, thinking about how she felt in that position. *Vulnerable*. That was the single word that captured what she was feeling. To follow Jesus Christ involves trusting that a life with greater vulnerability is richer and that opening ourselves in risky embrace is not irresponsible, but life-giving.

One Person

Poverty, hunger, war, disease, the suffering caused by natural disasters, addiction, racism, abuse, crime, environmental threat, lack of access to education and healthcare—the challenges are overwhelming, intransigent, impenetrable. They are too big and we are too small. What good can one person possibly accomplish? Do the efforts of like-minded people have any impact?

Imagine that Jennifer, a suburban professional woman in her twenties, prayerfully discerns God's call to focus on alleviating hunger, one of the most complex challenges. Can one person make a difference?

Jennifer studies the root causes of hunger, the international policies that lead to shortages or surpluses, the sustainability of agricultural practices, and consumer patterns. She re-examines her own patterns of shopping and eating. If every person consumed as she does, would the situation improve or deteriorate? Every dollar she spends contributes to the solution or to the problem, and

this knowledge becomes a tool for conscientious change. As she connects her personal practices to patterns of land use, fairness in trading, and global trends, she's empowered as a consumer. She adopts a lifestyle more conducive to the alleviation of hunger. Change starts with her.

As she feels more competent about issues that affect hunger, her knowledge shapes how she votes. She advocates for better policies with elected representatives. She makes connections to others who share her passion, and her collaboration gives her a stronger voice with decision-makers.

In Jennifer's professional work, she attends to questions about the impact her business practices have on people—on employees, communities, schools and young people, and on the environment. She connects what she has learned about hunger and influences corporate policies and practices in ways that help.

Next, she searches for opportunities to volunteer her time. A local food bank supplies resources to homeless

shelters for distribution. Nutrition programs in schools aim at children in poverty, community centers provide lunches for seniors, and Meals on Wheels ministries help the homebound. A new world opens up before her in her own community. Jennifer sees hunger first-hand in the eyes of people at an emergency shelter and listens to a mother who has no idea how she will feed her children the next day. She explores the work of the Red Cross and Heifer International. She finally commits to a particular social agency that does excellent work, and that needs her gifts. She feels at home with the other staff and volunteers. She offers her best.

She connects with people who share her passion. She speaks to church groups and teaches classes about hunger. She takes the youth group to visit service agencies. She serves on a congregation wide initiative to Africa. Her passion for alleviating hunger shapes her financial giving. And she prays daily for those who suffer from hunger as she invites God to show her other ways to make a difference.

Personal lifestyle changes, advocacy, hands-on volunteer service, teaching others, contributing money, prayer—there are hundreds of ways she can make a difference and impact hunger. The options are endless, and her passion fosters as many or as few activities as she has time and energy to fulfill.

Imagine that Jennifer pursues this calling with passion for the remainder of her life. Imagine forty or fifty years of learning, volunteering, leading, and contributing. Imagine that she deepens her knowledge and skill, and works more actively in some phases of life than in others as she balances this calling with work, family, and leisure. The cumulative impact is huge. Jennifer transforms the lives of hundreds of people locally and directly, invites and involves others through church and community, and strengthens agencies that help around the world.

With prayerful imagination, we can think of just as many personal responses to any challenge—abuse, violence, war, addiction, disease, poverty, education, healthcare. Any subcategory—literacy, Alzheimer 's, organ donation,

single parenting, immigration, alcoholism, depression—provides an array of opportunities by which one person can make a substantial difference. Through disciples following Jesus, God transforms the world.

If everyone thinks that nothing can be done, then nothing will be done. In ways mysterious beyond our comprehension, God multiplies our personal efforts, interweaves them with the work of others, and uses them to transform the world. This is fruitful living.

With the best of intentions, many followers of Christ help with a small project at the church every once in awhile. Service is sporadic, infrequent, and inconsistent. They dabble in doing good. But without focus, consistency, and persistence, we feel frustrated, awkward, and ineffective in serving. We're like students signing up for one tennis lesson, one piano lesson, one dance lesson, one woodworking lesson, and one swimming lesson; when we look back over time, we wonder why we've never mastered any of them. Competence and effectiveness in compassionate service derives from sustained effort through the periods of

feeling incompetent and awkward to the stages of practice, repetition, and nuanced learning to the advanced phases of graceful and fruitful expression.

Those who make the biggest difference take the long view. They practice. They learn. They grow in effectiveness. They persist. Like the river that cuts a great canyon through the rocks over millions of years, their effectiveness at changing overwhelming conditions derives from enduring, consistent, repeated, focused action.

With the scattering of seeds, a harvest presently unseen comes to fruition. Huge trees thrive where once a few seeds were planted by visionary and committed people. Compassionate service helps us discover a sense of purpose, a notion of personal mission.

The Covenant Prayer, composed and adapted by John Wesley, invites complete humility and obedience to God's service, asking God to work through us or to work around us, and to take us to places and put us alongside people we would never choose for ourselves.

THE COVENANT PRAYER

"I am no longer my own, but thine.

Put me to what thou wilt, rank me with whom thou wilt.

Put me to doing, put me to suffering.

Let me be employed by thee or laid aside for thee, exalted for thee or brought low by thee.

Let me be full, let me be empty.

Let me have all things, let me have nothing.

I freely and heartily yield all things to thy pleasure and disposal . . . ."[2]

With consistent practice, serving becomes integrated into our sense of self, a permanent part of our identity. We experience a sense of purpose that runs deep. Living with purpose means our life has a direction toward which we move that draws us forward despite difficulties, setbacks, and detours. Those who make a huge difference live with a palpable sense of purpose that is passionate, resilient, imaginative, vibrant, and persevering. It's contagious and inviting. It's as much a part of them as their personality or sense of humor. It becomes them. They become servants. They align with something true.

Nothing in the spiritual life adds so much satisfaction as truly making a positive difference in the lives of others. Serving others helps those we serve flourish; and we flourish in the serving of others.

REFLECTION

"Whenever you did one of these things to someone
OVERLOOKED *or* IGNORED,
that was ME
—YOU DID IT TO ME."

—*Matthew 25:40,* The Message

> *By serving others, we bear witness that Jesus' reality is true, that fullness is discovered in the giving and not in the taking; that abundance is found in loving rather than in fearing, that happiness comes in opening ourselves rather than by closing ourselves off.*

Questions

- How have you experienced Christ while serving? In yourself? In others?
- When have you moved out of your "comfort zone" in order to help another person?
- Read Wesley's Covenant Prayer again. What phrase speaks most clearly to you today?
- Where is the most unexpected place following Christ has ever taken you?
- Where have you seen God at work in the midst of loss and suffering? How have you been a part of God's work?

Prayer

Lord, help me to embrace a more vulnerable life. Teach me humility, courage, perseverance, discernment, and respect in my following you by serving others.

Loving and Serving Others

TRAINING THE HEART

If you only love the lovable, do you expect a pat on the back?...Help and give without expecting a return. You'll never—I promise—regret it.
—*Luke 6: 31-36* The Message

"What in the world am I doing here? I can't tell you how many times I've found myself asking that question." That's how Ken tells about the unexpected places his faith journey has taken him. Ken is a medical technician in his mid-fifties, a husband and father, a tennis player, and a handyman. He belongs to a congregation where he has attended worship for more than twenty-five years. He first helped with the Thanksgiving baskets, gathering canned goods and perishables and delivering boxes to families in need. Then Ken worked with the youth group on a week-long housing rehab project.

Later Ken received training and led a work team to Nicaragua where they rebuilt a school damaged by a hurricane, and they taught children. Now he mentors new members who want to get involved with hands-on service projects. "I never imagined myself doing this," he says. "But it answers the question, *What in the world am I here for*? This is the reason God put me here."

Ken followed a path that fit his gifts, context, and passions. Other peoples' pathways differ dramatically, and yet they follow a similar trajectory. Followers say *Yes* and

help in small ways with a project. They catch the spirit, noticing the difference their work makes for others and for themselves. They mature and gain confidence, branch out or deepen their commitment, and with time and a pattern of consistent service, they end up somewhere totally unexpected. Their own inner maturing in Christ makes a difference in the lives of other people and transforms the world.

Shirley's volunteer stint for a women's shelter led to repeated patterns of helping that opened the door for her work on their board of directors. This fed other passions she had, and she used her board-acquired skills to support literacy for children, which led her to teach volunteers at a literacy center, which has led to her involvement in school district educational initiatives.

Ana's volunteer teaching of elementary classes for Sunday school and vacation Bible school led to her helping with a weeklong VBS program in cooperation with an inner city church that reaches out to families with single moms. She loved it and formed relationships with the moms that led to her volunteer work in a jobs training program

and the establishment of an urban child-care program to support working single moms.

After Lance's retirement, he helped with a "clean up day" around the church with other retirees. He enjoys working outdoors with his hands, and he saw the need for more consistent care and repair of the church facilities. He and a friend worked together twice a month, trimming trees, planting bushes, painting doors, fixing leaks. He was invited to serve on the Grounds Committee. Lance was asked his opinion about the grounds at the community cemetery that had fallen into disrepair. Now he tends the cemetery, recruiting other retirees to help.

Ruth was in her late seventies when her husband died and she fell into a severe depression. The pastor encouraged her to visit her doctor and invited her to volunteer in the church office. She rediscovered long-neglected skills she had developed as an office worker decades before, and organized tasks in ways that helped the church. She became the support person for the mission volunteers who rebuild houses, feed the homeless, and visit shut-ins.

Earl was new to the faith when he attended a *Walk to Emmaus* retreat. He experienced a powerful personal transformation that led him to volunteer with future retreats. After two years of supporting and leading *Emmaus*, he felt called to help with *Kairos* prison-based retreats. He served on a planning team and then spent a weekend locked down with inmates to offer the retreat for them. He became active both with victims' rights organizations and prison reform agencies.

Jan has a career that takes her on the road constantly. With more than a hundred flights each year, her job does not allow her to embed herself into the community the way Ruth has, or to commit to regular volunteer service as Shirley does. How could she practice compassionate service? That was on her mind as she visited with the director of a hospice program that had helped her aunt during her terminal illness. Jan offered suggestions to improve the program's website and communications. Eventually, she served as an advisor to the director, regularly exchanging ideas by email and phone. One patient particularly touched her, and with the family's permission, she made contact by phone.

This became her pattern, phoning daily to check in, listen, encourage, and pray. If you want to serve, a way opens.

Sondra occasionally used her nursing skills to support weekend projects at her urban church that has an active ministry for the homeless, for addicts, and for people living with HIV. She served food at the shelter, distributed clothes, and assisted people in locating housing. She also raised money for her congregation's partner church in Mozambique. When she visited Mozambique, the experience changed her life. She became passionate about health issues in Africa, raising funds for malaria nets, organizing medical teams to work in Africa, and working as an advocate on world health issues and the diseases of poverty. She has spoken to dozens of churches and helped other people serve the poorest of the poor.

What in the world am I doing here? One thing leads to another and leads to another. With a disciplined pattern of serving and of opening themselves afresh to following Christ, all of these persons have ended up somewhere they could never have imagined. They each make a real

difference in the lives of others, and they are changing the part of the world God has given them to transform.

Risk-Taking Mission and Service changes the lives of those who offer ministry. It changes the lives of those who receive ministry. It changes the world as we share directly with God in the creating and re-creating work that makes all things new.

Start anywhere and at any time. It is never too late. And with continued cultivation and with the passage of time, the difference we make multiplies and the sense of satisfaction we experience deepens. When we answer Jesus' call, "Follow me," there's no predicting where we will end up!

Each person's work is like a seed, taking root, sprouting, breaking the surface, branching out, blossoming, and eventually casting other seeds to other places and becoming fruitful in ways beyond measure. Such stories are repeated in congregations and communities throughout the world. A follower responds to an invitation, a response made possible by the interior work that prepares them to act

boldly. With continued practice they experience an internal shift in priorities, subtle redirections of effort, slight corrections of course that help them find the right place and right work that God calls them to fulfill. Their personal passions and strengths become relevant for addressing human need. Serving involves trusting Christ and taking the next step, and the next, one after another.

Such fruitfulness may appear unachievable. Many of these stories took ten or twenty years to unfold. Incremental steps, persistence, passion, and time take us from here to there.

We may look at these examples with a guilty sense of repugnance. We may not admit it, but we don't even want to want to do some of these ministries—hospice care, soup kitchens, Third World countries. But these examples do not describe your path; you may be called to make a difference in an entirely different way. These are not prescribed paths; rather they stimulate our thinking and discernment. Many of these people felt the same way when they began. Their tastes, interests, desires, and tolerances have adapted from the beginning of their journeys until now. They didn't start by wanting these outcomes for themselves. They embrace situations now that they would have avoided at an earlier time, and they are now mystified by their former disgust. That's typical of God's calling

An Outward-Focused Life

Service refers to the volunteer impulse animated by the Spirit of God that causes people to offer their time, energy, and leadership to help their congregations and communities thrive. Through service, we become "doers of the word, and not merely hearers" (James 1:22), putting our faith into practice in concrete and visible ways. The church fulfills its mission through the active, altruistic, generous offering of mind, muscle, and spirit by people who sing in choirs, chair committees, manage rummage sales, assist with ushering, visit homebound members, coach soccer, paint the classrooms, and greet visitors. Service strengthens congregations and changes the lives of those who offer it.

Mission turns service outward and focuses beyond the walls of the congregation. Mission extends God's love to

the people of the community, the nation, and the world, and refers to the positive difference we make in the lives of others, whether or not they will ever become part of the community of faith. Mission involves our deliberate effort to improve the conditions of others; to relieve suffering; confront injustice; heal disease; and assist during times of crisis, loss, or grief. Mission pulls us out of ourselves and connects us with people we don't know. Service and mission are grace-driven, propelled by God's love for all people.

Jesus pushes us to extend our empathy to those not already in our circle of concern, and invites us to inspire others to do the same. "Here's a simple rule of thumb for your behavior: Ask yourself what you want people to do for you; then grab the initiative and do it for *them*! If you only love the lovable, do you expect a pat on the back? . . . Help and give without expecting a return. You'll never— I promise—regret it" (Luke 6:31-36, *The Message*).

An outward-focused life flows naturally and inescapably from following Christ, and early followers visited the sick

and the imprisoned, provided resources for the poor and vulnerable, reached out to people in need and drew them in by the grace of God. An initiating and active grace put love into action and bore witness to the world of the living Christ. To live "in Christ" means not only are we sustained by the presence of God's love revealed in Christ, but that the Spirit of Christ permeates us and motivates us to serve. "In Christ" means our identity derives from full-bodied openness to Jesus' way. Our faith in Christ proves its relevance in how we treat others.

If these vigorous practices represent mission and service, why modify the expectation with *Risk-Taking*? The practice of Risk-Taking Mission and Service pushes us out of our comfort zone and into places we would never go on our own. Those who practice Risk-Taking Mission and Service place themselves in situations that will change their minds. They voluntarily set aside their own convenience for a higher purpose. They follow Jesus into areas they would not tread on their own volition. They practice service with passion and intentionality, pouring themselves out for others. They go where Jesus leads, even when

it is uncomfortable, awkward, unexpected, and costly. They risk.

At the moment we face human suffering, a choice presents itself. If we pay careful attention to our natural tendencies, we discover that we desire to move away. We want to avoid pain, to deny the problem, to turn the other way. We are pulled toward safety. Fear and anxiety move us to secure and predictable territory.

If we listen deep within our soul, we discover that something inside us also draws us toward the suffering. Every human soul that harbors the tendency to avoid suffering also houses the capacity to respond compassionately. One path compels us away from pain; the other evokes the desire to help.

If we move toward suffering rather than running from it, we experience uncomfortable moments and awkward incidents. We risk feeling helpless, or worse, we risk sharing the pain of the person who suffers. Opening ourselves is

A TEACHER'S LESSON

One rainy night I started up the stairwell to my seminary apartment when I encountered one of my theology professors. Dr. D. was one of the most respected theologians of his generation, and I was completely surprised to see him in a student dorm. Dressed in his suit and tie from his day's teaching and covered by a wet overcoat, he was carrying bags of groceries up the stairs. I offered to help, and as we walked together I heard the story. The wife of a student had become gravely ill and was undergoing cancer treatment. They had been much in our prayers. Dr. D. had visited with them, and offered to help in any way he could. As a result, he went shopping for them after he finished his classes. He'd been doing this for weeks. Nothing I learned from him in the courses he taught had as much personal impact on me as finding him in that staircase on a cold, rainy night.

listening to someone share their loss without changing the subject; walking into a nursing home full of rancid smells and remaining there long enough to show that someone still cares; listening to people of different races tell us we will never be able to understand them; standing alongside people in their struggles to overcome, rebuild, and heal. It leaves us vulnerable.

God's call moves Jesus' disciples toward people in distress. In the Letter of James, we find, "Religion that is pure and undefiled . . . is this: to care for orphans and widows in their distress" (James 1:27). Visiting the sick, the suffering, the unjustly treated, and the lost is not possible if we follow our own inclinations, living by fear rather than by love.

At the crucial moment in our encounter with suffering (crucial moment literally means "the moment of the cross") when we decide whether to move away or toward it, following Jesus inevitably moves us toward people. Turning toward suffering is a moment of grace, the gift-like initiating love of God streams through us. Love defeats

fear, life overcomes death, compassion stands victorious over estrangement.

When we reach toward another, a new birth takes place, the creative dynamic of the Holy Spirit binds us together.

Training the heart to follow Christ involves learning to overcome fear. We acknowledge it and understand it, but choose to live by love instead. As we feed the impulses to act with love by consistent practice, we find courage to do things we would not otherwise do.Practices bring overwhelming tasks into manageable scope, reducing unreachable challenges to a size that is embraceable and doable. Practices involve steps that we take with consistency and frequency that lead us where we need to go. No one can face world hunger with confidence. But we can serve at the soup kitchen twice a month, write a congressional representative twice a year, and contribute to a reputable charity annually. We decide that the deliberate action is worth the effort.

Many times we know the right thing to do, but where can we find the courage to act? Our relationship with God and the community of Christ fosters confidence and hope. Risk-Taking Mission and Service are where courage and joy intermingle.

God's Spirit turns dentists into team leaders for Habitat for Humanity, school teachers into clinic hosts, store clerks into language tutors, accountants into Big Brothers, stay-at-home mothers into lobbyists for legislation that protects the uninsured, college professors into volunteer prison chaplains, car salesmen into cooks for mission teams, retired folks into literacy tutors, and can change you into something you can't now imagine.

Are you willing to put yourself in a situation that may cause you to change your mind?

REFLECTION

DON'T FOOL YOURSELF
into thinking that you are a listener when you are anything but, letting the Word go in one ear and out the other.

ACT ON WHAT YOU HEAR!
Those who hear and don't act are like those who glance in the mirror, walk away, and two minutes later have no idea who they are, what they look like.

—*James* 1:22-24, The Message

Start anywhere and at any time. It is never too late. When we answer Jesus' call, "Follow me," there's no predicting where we will end up!

Questions

- Can you think of a time when you felt a renewed sense of purpose and meaning in your life? What gifts were you using? What results were you helping to achieve?

- When has your participation in serving others caused you to change your mind about someone? How did you understand the person or the situation differently after becoming engaged with the context?

- Think again about the question from the first chapter. What particular gifts, abilities, or experiences prepare you to make a positive difference personally or in your community?

Prayer

Help me live for others, Christ, as you have lived and died for me. Remain at my side as you push me toward people who need your sustaining presence.

SOCIAL WITNESS

*What does the LORD require of you
but to do justice, and to love kindness,
and to walk humbly with your God?
—Micah 6:8*

Feeding one person at a time, visiting one prisoner at a time, and building one house at a time are vitally important. Hands-on, face-to-face ministry changes lives. The grace of God flows from person to person through life-changing mission. However, people who practice Risk-Taking Mission and Service also discern God's call to involve themselves in social change, political activity, and community causes. Some people offer themselves to change systems, confront injustice, and relieve suffering on a larger scale. The tools for change become policies, funding initiatives, and petitions rather than hammers, cooking pans, and wheelchair ramps. The imperative of God's love propels people into the struggle for change at all levels—personal, family, congregational, community, national, and global.

John Wesley's *inner holiness*, the sanctifying and perfecting love at work inside us, finds outward expression in *social witness*, a dedicated commitment to changing conditions that rob people of fullness of life. Social witness serves God, who is the "lover of justice" (Psalm 99:4). To have in us the mind that is in Christ means we perceive God's activity not

merely in stories of personal transformation but in the great shifts of history toward justice, release from oppression, and relief from suffering.

"Justice is love with legs," one seminary professor said. God's love takes a social form, a political expression, when the followers of Jesus learn to love strangers by relieving suffering through programs that prevent diseases, healthcare systems that serve all people, and labor policies that are fair. Social justice ministries seek the conversion of social structures toward greater justice, helping people to flourish.

Victims of violence, poverty, discrimination, and people who suffer through war, famine, or natural disaster often lack the power to effect change that will relieve them or transform their circumstance. If no one with power and resources speaks for them or stands with them, how can their voices be heard? To advocate means to speak for, to act on behalf of, to give support. Among the most important ways followers of Christ express God's gracious love is through advocacy, speaking for the children, the

oppressed, the homeless, the poor, and the marginalized who cannot speak for themselves.

As followers of Jesus, we look at the world through the perspective of someone who suffered innocently—a person who was crushed and broken by the world's powers—rather than through the lens of privilege, power, and wealth. Christianity began with catastrophic brokenness and violence, resulting in a persevering, sacrificial love that drives us to work on behalf of the suffering with unending passion. We can do no other. To follow Jesus in first- century Palestine meant walking into the caves of lepers, confronting violence against women, embracing children, exposing self-serving judges, condemning money changers, and challenging the indifference of the wealthy toward the poor and vulnerable. To follow Jesus today involves walking into HIV clinics, confronting abuse of power by government officials, challenging corporate greed and unfair labor practices, praying for peace, and supporting healthcare for children.

Social change is risky. Some social witness the world understands—seeking cures for cancer, protecting children

"I NEVER WOULD HAVE CHOSEN THIS FOR MYSELF"

Frank was an active church member in the 1960s when his daughter was arrested for drug possession in a foreign country. Her arrest happened at a critical time in the country's internal politics. They made an example of her, and she was unexpectedly sentenced to years of hard labor. Thus began Frank's several-year saga of personal pleadings, meetings with diplomats and policy-makers, and exposure to the extreme conditions of prison systems. He found support from his community of faith and the teachings of Scripture. The witness of Amnesty International motivated him to continue his service and advocacy long after his own daughter's release. For more than thirty years he directed his energies to creating more humane criminal justice systems, establishing treaties to eliminate torture and to abolish the death penalty. "I never would have chosen this for myself," he says, "but given what happened to my family, I felt called to do all I could." Victims become survivors by discovering the inner calling of God to turn their personal suffering into channels for connecting with others for the transformation of the world.

from abuse, supporting victims of violence. Other forms of social witness the world cannot fathom because the ideas run counter to deep cultural biases or because such initiatives seem foolish, unrealistic, or hopeless—working with violent offenders, protesting torture, establishing programs for drug addicts, organizing for peace, protecting the rights of immigrants. Public opinion stoked by moral conviction can leverage powerful change.

Most of the people reading this book are the beneficiaries of various forms of privilege. Most of us have enjoyed opportunities to make a living; live freely; feel protected by the law; and benefit from medical, financial, and educational institutions. Most of us have probably made conscientious choices based on good motives. We do our best.

Yet some of the benefits we enjoy have derived from belonging to systems that hurt the planet, take advantage of the poor, or depend upon oppressive labor practices in foreign countries. Some of the opportunities we have enjoyed were closed to others for no reasons other than race, nationality, or financial advantage. People can live personally responsible and moral lives while also

unknowingly or unwillingly participating in systems that are immoral or hurtful.

Prophetic voices help us see the incongruity between what we believe and the personal choices we actually make. The dissonance is uncomfortable. We want such voices to be wrong, even when we intuitively know that some of what they say is true. Listening attentively rather than reacting with indignation may cause us to rethink and to act with greater fairness and more compassion. Then we are able to influence systems and make personal choices that align more truly to the deep principles we hold. God speaks to us sometimes through the voices of people who disagree with us and who really irritate us just as the prophets of the Old Testament bothered the comfortable, complacent, wealthy, and powerful in days gone by. They rally us to a necessary collective sense of responsibility.

Part of the hard inner work of perceiving God's activity involves developing a social consciousness, a heightened awareness of how our lives interconnect with others in positive as well as hurtful ways. Belonging to a community,

working for a company, or enjoying the benefits of citizenship involves taking responsibility for their directions, policies, and practices. How can we do less harm and more good? How do we have in us the mind that is in Christ Jesus? is a social question as well as a personal one.

In following Christ, one of the greatest risks is the sin of omission, failing to do the things we ought to do. Sometimes we know what is right, but a lack of courage or a failure of nerve makes us afraid to act. Our self-interest and unwillingness to act are offensive to God. With any social justice initiative, people will disagree, resist, and push back. Conscientious people we love and respect will disagree with us. Effective work requires humility, grounding in Christ, a willingness to listen and to learn, and a positive perseverance.

People are hungry for what makes a positive difference. Some find their place in personal, hands-on, face-to-face contact. Others find themselves called by God to offer themselves as change agents at the public, corporate, or policy level. Both deserve our prayerful support and discernment. We are personal disciples and social

creatures, and God's grace leads us to private action and public change. God forms us in the way of Christ for the transformation of the world.

Famine is real. Disease is real. Devastating birth defects caused by toxins in the environment are real.

Killing is real. Addiction, desperation, violence, and poverty are real.

In a world where these things are real, what kind of person do you want to be? What kind of person do you think God wants you to be?

The Practice of Risk-Taking Mission and Service

People who practice Risk-Taking Mission and Service understand obedience to Christ. Some things they do, not because they enjoy it, but because Jesus Christ would do it, invites them to do it, or commands them to do it. They go where Jesus goes.

They improve on how to have a greater impact. They become progressively more strategic in their service,

THE WORLD GOD HAS GIVEN YOU

Mr. Martinez is in his eighties and has been a follower of Christ for more than sixty years. He is nearly blind and has a hard time getting around on his own. Twice each week his daughter drives him to a retirement home where he visits and cares for six fellow church members. Some of them are longtime friends, and others were identified by the pastor as needing support. He reads the paper with them, helps them with their mail, brings them books, watches baseball with them, and prays for them. He provides a rich ministry. He takes it seriously, and it makes a huge difference. The part of the world God has given Mr. Martinez to transform is a single retirement center.

God uses the church to make disciples of Jesus Christ for the transformation of the world. What portion of the world has God given you to transform?

learning to maximize effectiveness and fruitfulness. They learn to serve.

Whether their service involves bricks and mortar, soup kitchen lunches or blanket distribution, money-raising or legislative initiative, they consciously focus on the people being served. They treat people with dignity. They see the face of Christ in those they serve, and they represent the grace of God in their serving. They do not patronize.

They saturate their work with prayer, finding strength, grounding, motivation, and calling in their relationship with God. Through serving, they discover God; through God, they discover serving.

They do not think more highly of themselves than they ought to think. They practice humility. The difference they make comes from God.

They live their spiritual convictions, examining whether what they do in their employment is consistent with their desire to serve God and others. They avoid harmful practices that take advantage of the poor or which further

violate or damage the earth. They strive to eliminate prejudices such as those related to race, religion, gender, nationality, age, or economic condition from their own lives and workplaces. They promote justice, and their lives give testimony to the fair treatment of people and a concern for the disadvantaged. They practice God's new creation.

They treat well those whom society seems to think it's all right to mistreat—maids, waiters, cash register attendants, ticket counter people, store shelvers, custodians, street vendors, people of other nationalities, groundskeepers, and others in the service industry. Serving Christ is not merely about major projects and coordinated work teams, but about one-on-one, person-to-person respect, courtesy, and helpfulness. They listen. They notice people whom others overlook. They express appreciation. They treat people the way they would want to be treated.

People who serve in the Spirit of Christ do not demean or dismiss people by ignoring them. They serve expecting nothing in return, and they do not offer gifts that impose a burden or dependency. Their service doesn't exact a cost in dignity from those who receive.

They never regard people as objects, things, or statistics. When they serve on medical and construction teams, they do not treat people as soulless bodies. When they serve on worship, teaching, and pastoral care teams, they do not treat people as bodiless souls.

They *practice* serving. Serving is something learned, and there are no instant experts. They begin small, anticipate feelings of temporary incompetence, and they build up their "serving muscles." They practice when it's easier not to; they overcome internal resistances and external criticism; they serve when they feel awkward and clumsy doing it; they do it with others and learn from mentors; they never stop serving until they feel confident, graceful, and natural doing it. They become servants.

Those who practice Risk-Taking Mission and Service take the long view, knowing that the conditions that cause suffering— poverty, disease, violence, hunger—do not arise overnight and they are not solved quickly. They do not lose hope. They never give up. They persist.

They approach the suffering of other people with both awe and joy. They walk gently with those who are vulnerable.

They expand boundaries to get the job done. They work with other churches, other denominations, non-church and governmental agencies, and businesses to help people in need. The work of the Holy Spirit is not confined to those who call it by that name. They collaborate.

People who serve Christ by serving others don't go it alone. They immerse themselves in community. They've inherited their ministry from others and will pass it along to others; they balance one another's weaknesses and strengths. They do not insist on their own way. They submit willingly to the wisdom of the body of Christ.

They do not avoid the hard tasks, the unsolvable problems, the persistent challenges.

They are more interested in impacting lives in positive ways than in receiving credit. They easily express appreciation to others and give thanks to God.

They accept the uncertainty of outcomes. When addicts return to their drugs, newly constructed houses are flooded

again, scholarship recipients drop out of school, or parolees steal from the soup kitchen, they persevere. They scatter more seeds. They mature from "what's in it for me?" to "how can I help?" and from "they ought" to "I will." They find a way. Nobody is too far away, no village too remote, no obstacles too large, no resistance too severe that they can't figure out some way to make a positive difference. They connect, collaborate, negotiate, think, plan, borrow, strategize, and push until a way opens.

They take hardship, resistance, setback, and disappointment in stride, knowing that if serving people was always easy, fun, and convenient, then it wouldn't have taken Christ to teach us, and he wouldn't have told us about taking up crosses.

They invite young people to serve alongside them, share their experiences with children, and teach the next generation how to serve.

They turn over the reins of leadership when the time is ripe. They mobilize others to meet human needs. They

inspire and lead and teach. They do not coerce or use guilt. They invite and support. They help people take first steps.

People who serve in Christ's name evaluate projects in order to improve their ministries so that they become more fruitful. They invite feedback. They do better with each project. They excel in doing good.

They honor service in many forms—hands-on, policy-oriented, social activism, service on boards, personal engagement, charitable donation. They respect those who are out front as well as those who work behind the scenes.

They don't merely pray for peace; they work for it.

REFLECTION

Then Jesus went to work on his disciples. . . .

"Don't run from suffering; **EMBRACE IT.**

FOLLOW ME *and* **I'LL SHOW YOU HOW.**

Self-help is no help at all.

SELF- SACRIFICE *is the way,*

MY WAY, *to finding yourself,*

YOUR TRUE SELF."

—Matthew 16:24-25, The Message

How can we do less harm and more good? How do we have in us the mind that is in Christ Jesus? *is a social question as well as a personal one.*

Loving and Serving Others

Questions

- What do you consider the three most critical issues that require response and service to improve the human condition and relieve suffering?

- In these three areas, where do you see yourself fitting in and making a difference?

- What's the one thing you know you can do, that if you did it frequently and consistently, would have the greatest positive effect on the life of people in your community?

Prayer

May I never feel embarrassed to speak for you, Jesus, or to act on the behalf of those who suffer. Remain at my side as you push me toward people who need your sustaining presence. Help me live for others, Christ, as you have lived and died for me.

Leader Helps
for Small Group Sessions

Loving and Serving Others

SESSION 1: *Why Serve Others?*
Focus Point: There are various common motivations for serving others, and the Holy Spirit purifies them all when we serve with the right spirit and focus, serving the purposes of Christ.

GETTING READY *(Prior to the Session)*

Preparation for each session:
• Read Chapter 1 in *Loving and Serving Others*.
• Write the key Scripture and focus point on a board or chart.
• Review Digging In and Making Application, and select the points and discussion questions you will cover.
• Acquire a box of index cards and a bag of pens.
• Pray for the session and for your group members.

Key Scripture: *For those who want to save their life will lose it, and those who lose their life for my sake, and for the sake of the gospel, will save it. Mark 8:35*

Main Ideas:
• Serving others and making a difference in the world is key to a satisfying life.
• Common motivations for serving others are a sense of duty, contributing to the social fabric of human life and personal satisfaction.

GETTING STARTED

Opening Prayer
Compassionate and loving God, you have designed us in such a way that we discover our true selves when we give ourselves to others. Help us to serve others. Use us to accomplish your work, transforming lives and the world. Amen.

DIGGING IN

Begin by pointing out that we tend to live to ourselves. We are focused on our private concerns, personal passions, hobbies, entertainments, family responsibilities, and work obligations. The culture in which we live bombards us with messages such as "Look out for number one," "Love yourself first," and "People are responsible for their own misfortunes."
Read the following quotation aloud:
"Most people, given the choice between having a better world, or a better place within the world as it is, would choose the latter."

Group Discussion
• Given our self-centered tendencies, how do you think anyone learns to serve? How did you learn to serve?
• What is your earliest memory of helping others as an expression of your faith?

Review the common motivations people can have for serving others from the chapter.
Group Discussion
• What motivates you to serve?
• Where do your unmet needs intersect with your own personal passions? What particular gifts, abilities, or experiences prepare you to make a positive difference—personally, in your community, and in the world?

MAKING APPLICATION

What Does It Look Like?
Read aloud the following excerpt from Chapter 1 that begins, "Since time immemorial, prophets and religious leaders, philosophers and poets, . . . " (p. 19)
Briefly discuss:
• Why is serving others a critical key to a purposeful life?
• Why should we serve or help others?

Hand out note cards and pens to each participant. Ask them to write the following questions along with their answers on their note cards. These answers will not be shared, but encourage them to keep this card in their Bibles or books and bring them each week as they will add to the list.
• What is your current level of regularly serving others?
• How can your passions, skills, and experiences meet a need?

What Now?
Instruct participants to reflect silently in response to this question:
• In light of all we have shared today, what do you sense God saying to you?

End by inviting answers to these questions:
• In response, what will you do differently this week?
• How will what you learned this week change how you live your life?

Close your session with prayer requests and invite a participant to close in prayer.

Loving and Serving Others

SESSION 2: *An Essential Truth*

Focus Point: We discover ourselves and become the persons God created us to be when we give ourselves to others in Christ-like service.

GETTING READY *(Prior to the Session)*

Key Scripture: *Jesus said, "Whoever wants to be great must become a servant. . . . That is what the Son of Man has done: He came to serve, not be served—and then to give away his life. . ." (Matthew 20:27-28,* The Message).

Main Ideas
- In Christ, we discover that the truest reality of all is that we are interconnected. We belong to one another because we all belong to God.
- We become the persons God created us to be when we give ourselves to others in Christ-like service.

GETTING STARTED

Opening Prayer
Compassionate and loving God, you have designed to discover our true selves when we give ourselves to others. Use us to accomplish your work in the world. Amen.

DIGGING IN

Present the idea that we are all interconnect, and that when we come to this realization, we are propelled to the highest and truest of responses. If we allow the person in the burning building to die something within us dies.

Group Discussion
- Think of a time when you responded to the need of a stranger or someone you did not know well. What prompted you to help? Did you experience a sense of connection with the individual? Describe how you felt during and after the experience.
- What are some small ways you pour out your life to others each day?

Have someone read aloud the following Scriptures: Romans 14:7-8; Matthew 25:40; and Mark 8:35.
Then read aloud the following quote from Chapter 2: "Serving others does not merely involve helpful activities that make a difference; Christ-like service helps us become the persons God created us to be" (p. 34).

Group Discussion
• How does Christ-like service help us to become the persons God created us to be?
• What experiences of serving have helped you to discover your true self?

MAKING APPLICATION

What Does It Look Like?
Review Jennifer's story from Chapter 2 and highlight how one person can make a substantial difference (p. 40-43).
Briefly discuss:
• How does God multiply our efforts, interweaving them with the work of others, to transform the world? Share a way that God has multiplied your efforts to make a difference.
• What does it mean to say that effective service requires practice and persistence?
• How does consistent practice make serving a part of our identity? How has consistent serving helped to shape your identity and direction in life? How has it added to your sense of satisfaction in life?

Wrap up the session by reading aloud Wesley's Covenant Prayer (p. 46).

Tell participants to pull out their note cards from last week. Ask them to write two new questions along with their answers on their note cards. These answers will not be shared, but encourage them to keep this card in their Bibles or books and bring them each week as they will add to the list.
• What would your life look like if this was your prayer?
• What would it take for this prayer to be a true desire of your heart?

What Now?
Instruct participants to reflect silently in response to this question:
• In light of all we have shared today, what do you sense God saying to you?

End by inviting answers to these questions:
• In response, what will you do differently this week?
• How will what you learned this week change how you live your life?

Close your session with prayer requests and invite a participant to close in prayer.

SESSION 3: *Training the Heart*

Focus Point: The practice of Risk-Taking Mission and Service pushes us out of our comfort zone and into places we would never go on our own, which involves learning to overcome fear.

GETTING READY *(Prior to the Session)*

Key Scripture: *If you only love the lovable, do you expect a pat on the back?...Help and give without expecting a return. You'll never—I promise—regret it.* Luke 6: 32, 36 The Message

Main Ideas:
• Risk-Taking Mission and Service changes lives—both of those who offer service and of those who receive it—and transforms the world.
• The practice of Risk-Taking Mission and Service pushes us out of our comfort zone and into places we would never go on our own, which involves learning to overcome fear.

GETTING STARTED

Opening Prayer
Compassionate and loving God, Help us to serve others, transforming lives and the world. Amen.

DIGGING IN

Read aloud the excerpt from Chapter 3 beginning, "At the moment we face human suffering, a choice presents itself" (p. 62).

Group Discussion
• When have you moved out of your "comfort zone" in order to help another person?
• What has been "risk-taking" about your service to Christ?
• What helps you to overcome your fears so that you may follow Christ regardless of the risks or cost?

Refer to the section, "An Outward Focused Life". Read the two-paragraph excerpt that begin, "Service refers to the volunteer impulse animated by the Spirit of God ..."

Group Discussion
• How would you articulate the difference between service and mission?
• What opportunities have you had to serve?
• What opportunities have you had to be in mission?

The Practice of Risk-Taking Mission and Service

MAKING APPLICATION

What Does It Look Like?
Read the excerpt from Chapter 3 that begins, "God's Spirit turns dentists into team leaders for Habitat for Humanity…" (p. 66).

Briefly discuss:
• Are you willing to put yourself in a situation that may cause you to change your mind? Read aloud the key Scripture verse:
• If you only love the lovable, do you expect a pat on the back?…Help and give without expecting a return. You'll never—I promise—regret it. Luke 6: 32, 36 *The Message*

Ask participants to pull out their note cards from last week. Ask them to write two new questions along with their answers on their note cards. These answers will not be shared, but encourage them to keep this card in their Bibles or books and bring them each week as they will add to the list.
• When have you been guiltily of only loving the lovable?
• How can you take more risks with mission and service?

What Now?
Instruct participants to reflect silently in response to this question:
• In light of all we have shared today, what do you sense God saying to you?

End by inviting answers to these questions:
• In response, what will you do differently this week?
• How will what you learned this week change how you live your life?

Close your session with prayer requests and invite a participant to close in prayer.

Loving and Serving Others

Focus Point: People who practice Risk-Taking Mission and Service understand obedience to Christ. Some things they do, not because they enjoy it, but because Jesus Christ would do it, invites them to do it, or commands them to do it. They go where Jesus goes.

GETTING READY *(Prior to the Session)*

Key Scripture: *What does the Lord require of you but to do justice, and to love kindness, and to walk humbly with your God?" Micah 6:8*

Main Ideas:
- People who practice Risk-Taking Mission and Service also discern God's call to involve themselves in social change, political activity, and community causes.
- Among the most important ways we express God's love is through advocacy, speaking for the children, the oppressed, the homeless, the poor, and those who cannot speak for themselves.

GETTING STARTED

Opening Prayer
Compassionate and loving God, you have designed us in such a way that we discover our true selves when we give ourselves to others. Help us to serve others. Use us to accomplish your work, transforming lives and the world. Amen.

DIGGING IN

Direct participants to Chapter 4 to the section called The Practice of Risk-Taking Mission and Service. Highlight the habits or characteristics of people who practice Risk-Taking Mission and Service.

Group Discussion
- Why do you think these habits are critical to effective service?
- Which habits are more challenging for you, and why?
- Name some people in your congregation who exhibit these characteristics. Where, do you think, does his or her ability to take risks in mission and service come from?

Read the excerpt from Chapter 4 that begins, "Justice is love with legs," one seminary professor said" (p. 71).

Group Discussion
• Why should Christians care about justice and social issues?
• How has God's love taken form in social or political expression through followers of Jesus?
• What are some social justice issues in your community? in our world?
• How can we develop a social consciousness?
• What are some social justice issues in your community? in our world?

MAKING APPLICATION

What Does It Look Like?
Refer to the section in Chapter 4, The World God Has Given You (p. 78). Invite a volunteer to read it aloud to the group.
Briefly discuss:
• How have you seen God to use the church to transform the world?
• What portion of the world has God given you to transform?

Tell participants to pull out their note cards from last week. Ask them to write two new questions along with their answers on their note cards. These answers will not be shared, but encourage them to keep this card in their Bibles or books and review from time to time.
• What is "risk-taking" about your current level of service to your community, to the world?
• What patterns do I hope God will use to reshape my life? How will I begin these patterns/ practices?

What Now?
Instruct participants to reflect silently in response to this question:
• In light of all we have shared today, what do you sense God saying to you?

End by inviting answers to these questions:
• In response to these sessions on Risk-Taking Mission and Service what will you do differently this week?
• How will what you learned this week and in the book Loving and Serving Others: The Practice of Risk-Taking Mission and Service, change how you live your life?

Close your session with prayer requests and invite a participant to close in prayer.

Notes

1 Frederick Buechner, *Wishful Thinking* (HarperSanFrancisco, 1993); p.119

2 *The United Methodist Hymnal* (The United Methodist Publishing House, 1989); p. 607.